TENNESSEE

Past and Present

Diane Bailey

rosen publishing's
rosen
central®

New York

Published in 2010 by The Rosen Publishing Group, Inc.
29 East 21st Street, New York, NY 10010

First Edition

Library of Congress Cataloging-in-Publication Data

Bailey, Diane, 1966-
Tennessee: past and present / Diane Bailey.—1st ed.
    p. cm.—(The United States: past and present)
Includes bibliographical references and index.
ISBN 978-1-4358-3522-1 (library binding)
ISBN 978-1-4358-8494-6 (pbk)
ISBN 978-1-4358-8495-3 (6 pack)
1. Tennessee—Juvenile literature. I. Title.
F436.3.B35 2010
976.8—dc22

                                                    2009022966

Manufactured in the United States of America

CPSIA Compliance Information: Batch #LW10YA: For Further Information contact Rosen Publishing, New York, New York at 1-800-237-9932

On the cover: Top left: The Ryman Auditorium served as the home of the Grand Ole Opry until 1974. Top right: The Smoky Mountains get their name from the natural fog that often hangs over the range. Bottom: A trolley runs in downtown Memphis.

Contents

Introduction   5

Chapter 1
The Geography of Tennessee   6

Chapter 2
The History of Tennessee   12

Chapter 3
The Government of Tennessee   19

Chapter 4
The Economy of Tennessee   25

Chapter 5
**People from Tennessee:
Past and Present**   31

Timeline   38

Tennessee at a Glance   39

Glossary   41

For More Information   42

For Further Reading   45

Bibliography   46

Index   47

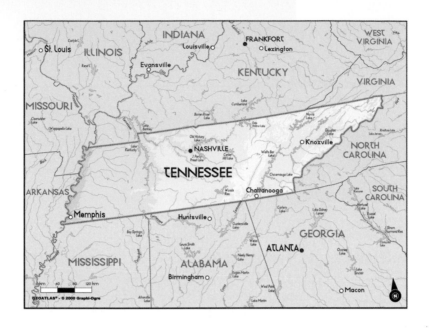

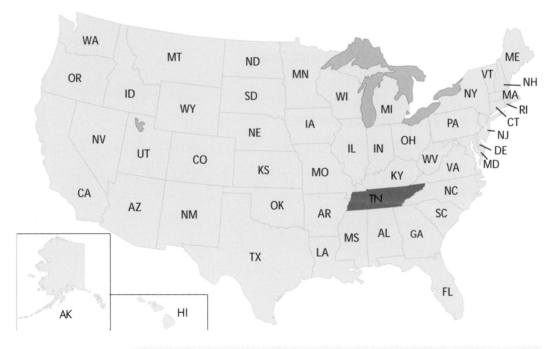

Tennessee's major cities are located in each of its three regions: East, Middle, and West. Tennessee is considered part of the southern United States.

Introduction

Tennessee is like the "roof" of the American South. It is a long rectangle that sits on top of Mississippi, Alabama, and Georgia. Tennessee's other neighbors are North Carolina, Virginia, Arkansas, and Kentucky. All the states surrounding Tennessee have contributed to its culture.

A good word to describe Tennessee's people is "individual." The state was built by people who were creative and capable. The first Tennesseans were people who made a life from the state's many natural resources.

Native Americans lived in Tennessee for thousands of years. In the 1700s, white settlers on the East Coast started to push westward. They reached the Appalachian Mountains. For many years, these settlers did not get much farther. The mountains were very difficult to cross. Eventually, some adventurous souls wanted to see what was on the other side. Long hunters were men who traveled long distances into the "overmountain" territories. They found that the rugged mountains in the East spread out into fertile fields in the West. They had found the land that would become Tennessee.

The state has a colorful history. Its people have been farmers and factory workers, musicians and military leaders, and pioneers and presidents. The state played an important part in the Civil War and the struggle for civil rights. It has helped shape the country that we live in today.

Chapter 1

THE GEOGRAPHY OF TENNESSEE

If you were to explore the ancient land of Tennessee, you would not need your hiking boots. You would need a boat! About five hundred million years ago, the "land" of Tennessee was covered by a huge, shallow ocean.

Under the water, the earth's crust was restless. Huge pieces of the earth's surface, called tectonic plates, crashed against each other. The force crumpled the pieces and pushed them upward. This process took a couple hundred million years. The result is what now forms most of East Tennessee: the Appalachian Mountains.

When it was new, this mountain range was probably twice as tall as it is now. Over time, the mountains have worn down. The Appalachians are among the oldest mountains on Earth. Sometimes, people will say something is as "old as the hills," but it's probably not quite as old as the Appalachian Mountains!

The Three States of Tennessee

Tennessee is divided into three parts—East, Middle, and West. Each section is very different from the others.

East Tennessee is full of mountains. The Unaka Mountains are part of the Appalachian mountain range. These mountains are often

Vivid autumn colors decorate the great Smoky Mountains in East Tennessee. The blue mist that settles in between the mountains gave them their name.

shrouded in a blue mist that looks like smoke. That's where they get their other name—the Smoky Mountains.

West of the Smoky Mountains is a thin strip of land that runs north to south. It is called the East Tennessee Valley and Ridge. The land here switches between ridges and valleys.

The Cumberland Plateau is a little farther to the west. It is about 50 miles (80 kilometers) wide, with steep cliffs on both its eastern and western sides. Early settlers had a hard time getting across the Cumberland Mountains. In 1750, an explorer found a pass through the mountains that had long been used by Native Americans. The "Cumberland Gap" became an important travel route.

After the Cumberland Plateau comes another plateau. This one is called the Highland Rim. It is shaped like a large bowl. The bowl circles the Central Basin, which is the lower part in the middle. The western edge of the Highland Rim bumps up against the Tennessee River. This river is the boundary between Middle and West Tennessee.

When the mountains of East Tennessee were being formed, the western third of the state actually sank. Sand and dirt washed down into it. This helped make the fertile soil of West Tennessee's farmland.

Rivers and Lakes

Three important rivers cut across the land of Tennessee. The Cumberland River runs across the north central part of the state. A beautiful point on the Cumberland River is Cumberland Falls. It is a waterfall that is 68 feet (20 meters) high. The Tennessee River runs through Tennessee not once, but twice! First it flows south through the eastern part of the state until it reaches Alabama. Then it turns back north and enters the state on the western side. The Mississippi River is even farther west. It forms the entire western boundary of the state.

Most of Tennessee's big lakes are man-made. Engineers built dams on the river to create them. However, one large lake in Tennessee is natural. Reelfoot Lake, in northwestern Tennessee, covers about 15,000 acres (6,070 hectares). A powerful earthquake in 1811 broke the land open. A large area sank. The force of the earthquake caused the Mississippi River to flow backward for a few minutes. It filled up the recently created bowl. The Mississippi River got back on track, but it left behind Reelfoot Lake. Bald cypress trees

Two hundred years ago, the New Madrid Earthquakes, a series of three powerful earthquakes, created Reelfoot Lake in northwestern Tennessee.

grow in the lake, and bald eagles live there. People like to fish and boat on the lake.

Natural Abundance

Tennessee is one of the most "biodiverse" states in the nation. This means there are lots of species of plants and animals. Forests of hardwood trees like oak, maple, and walnut grow throughout the state. American chestnut trees almost died out from disease in the early 1900s. However, some still thrive in Middle Tennessee. These surviving trees are being used to grow new ones.

Underground Tennessee

Past . . . .

Miles of caves wind under the hills of Tennessee. These caves were formed by underground streams that eroded the rock.

Four thousand years ago, the residents of Tennessee used these caves. They drew artwork on the cave walls. Early pictures were of simple objects like the sun and snakes. Later, people drew animals such as turtles and owls. There are also pictures of humans.

Some of these pictures were scratched into wet mud and then dried. This is the case at Mud Glyph Cave (a glyph is a marking). Some of the figures there date back to 465 CE.

Indian Cave and Devil Step Hollow Cave are in Middle Tennessee. These caves have petroglyphs on the walls. Petroglyphs are markings that are carved into rock. In other caves, Native Americans drew pictures with charcoal.

The Mississippian Indians lived in Tennessee from about 500 CE to 1500 CE. Some of their markings show that they probably used the caves for ceremonies. For example, the caves were sometimes used as burial places. These early Native Americans also collected minerals from the caves. Sometimes, they were just exploring.

And Present . . . .

Today, spelunkers explore Tennessee's many caves while armed with lights and ropes. They have discovered almost eight thousand caves in Tennessee.

The Lost Sea Caverns, which are filled with Native American artifacts, are now popular with tourists. This cave system has a 4.5-acre (1.5 ha) lake that is 300 feet (91 m) below the surface. It is the world's largest underground lake.

Cumberland Caverns is a network of caves that is 28 miles (45 km) long. It is one of the largest in the world. Today, visitors can also spend a night underground—but writing on the walls is not allowed!

Flowers grow everywhere in Tennessee. The Smoky Mountains have more than fifteen hundred different types of flowers. That's more than any other national park.

Early residents hunted small animals for food. Opossums, foxes, raccoons, and rabbits are always hiding in the hills and valleys of Tennessee. More than three hundred different kinds of birds live in Tennessee. Some animals that live in Tennessee are not found anywhere else in the country.

Several hundred black bears live in the Smoky Mountains. Black bears used to live all over the United States. Now, they have lost most of their habitat.

A black bear climbs an oak tree. Tennessee is one of the few places where black bears still live wild in the United States.

The Smoky Mountains are one of the few places they can still be found in the wild.

Underground, there are valuable deposits of coal, zinc, and limestone. Tennessee's rich natural resources have all helped in the state's development.

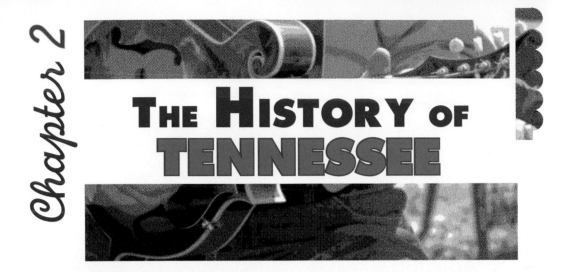

Chapter 2

THE HISTORY OF TENNESSEE

People have lived in Tennessee for about fifteen thousand years. The first Native Americans hunted animals and ate plants that grew naturally in Tennessee. Early Indians hunted large animals like mastodons. Later, the Indians hunted smaller animals and learned how to farm.

The first European to reach Tennessee was Hernando de Soto. He was a Spanish explorer who came to the Americas in 1540. Cherokee, Creek, and Chickasaw Indians lived in Tennessee at this time. More explorers and settlers arrived over the next two hundred years. Settlers wanting land clashed with the Native Americans who already lived there.

Settlers and Statehood

In the 1700s, the United States was a group of colonies. The colonies were governed by Great Britain. The current state of Tennessee was still part of North Carolina.

In 1763, the British government established the Proclamation Line. This boundary ran across the top of the Appalachian Mountains. The British government told settlers not to cross this line into the West. They did not want settlers and Native Americans getting into any more conflicts.

Many of Tennessee's early settlers crossed the Appalachian Mountains, even though the British government forbid it in an attempt to keep peace with the Indians.

However, some people from North Carolina were unhappy with the government. They wanted to move westward so that they would be out of the government's reach. The settlers also wanted more land for hunting and farming. Slowly, people trickled West.

The next twenty-five years brought many changes. The pioneers fought with Native Americans over land. The American Revolution started in 1775. Many Tennessee settlers joined the fight for independence.

After the war, they still had problems with North Carolina's government. In 1784, a group of settlers decided to break away. They formed the state of Franklin. It included part of the current state of

Rights for African Americans

Past ....

In 1865, in Pulaski, Tennessee, a group of men who had fought for the South started an organization. It was called the Ku Klux Klan (KKK). Members of the KKK opposed rights for black people. They bullied people and sometimes acted violently. The KKK was broken up in 1870 but came back again in 1915.

The struggle for civil rights continued in the twentieth century. In the 1950s and 1960s, African Americans began to stand up for their rights. Throughout the country, people did not agree on whether black people should be treated the same as whites. The people of Tennessee could not agree either.

The federal government said that both black and white children could go to the same schools. This was called integration, but it did not work in Tennessee. In Clinton, Tennessee, the black children came to school, and the white children stayed away. The civil rights movement was a painful process. Some demonstrations were peaceful. Others became violent.

Martin Luther King Jr., an African American minister, spoke in favor of equal rights. He came to Memphis in 1968 and stayed at the Lorraine Motel. While he stood on the balcony of his room, he was shot and killed. The civil rights movement continued after his death.

Present ....

The KKK still exists but does not have as much power as it used to. Rather than being one large organization, the KKK is made up of many small groups.

Today, the Lorraine Motel is the National Civil Rights Museum. About two hundred thousand people visit each year to learn about the long struggle for equal rights.

The struggle for civil rights continues today, not just in the South, but all over the United States.

Tennessee. However, the U.S. government did not accept the new state. Franklin's local government also had trouble, and after a while it returned to North Carolina.

Over the next fifteen years, however, the territory grew. Finally there were enough people to become a state. Tennessee joined the Union on June 1, 1796.

The People's President

Tennessee represented the best of frontier life: people worked hard and had a lot of individual freedom. They were loyal to their new country.

Andrew Jackson was Tennessee's first congressman, a senator, and a state supreme court judge before becoming U.S. president.

When the War of 1812 was fought between the British and the Americans, so many Tennessee soldiers joined this war that people called Tennessee the Volunteer State.

Tennessean Andrew Jackson was a commander in this war. He was so tough that people nicknamed him Old Hickory. In 1828, Jackson ran for president. He was not like previous presidents. His family was not wealthy, and he did not get much education. However, Jackson understood the problems of regular people, and he believed in the rights of the common man. He was called the people's president. Jackson was so popular that he served two terms. He started in 1828 and left office in 1837. One controversial thing he did was to sign the Indian Removal Act. This law ordered Native Americans to leave their homes in Tennessee. About sixteen thousand Cherokee Indians were forced to walk hundreds of miles to their new "home" in Oklahoma. About one-fourth of them died along the way. Because of their sadness and hardship, the route is called the "Trail of Tears."

Civil War

During the Civil War, the southern states fought against the northern states. The North wanted to end slavery. The South did not. Landowners in the South owned African American slaves who worked on huge plantations. If the owners did not use slaves, they would not make as much money. The argument got so bad that several southern states seceded (broke away) from the United States. The Civil War began.

Tennessee was caught in the middle. Farmers in the western part of the state used slaves. They sided with the South. East Tennessee was more sympathetic to the North. Eventually, Tennessee did secede from the Union, but it was the last state to do so. The state was still divided. Some Tennessee soldiers fought for the South. Others fought for the North.

The Battle of Shiloh was one of the Civil War's worst battles. It was fought in April 1862 in Hardin County, Tennessee. In just two days, the two sides combined suffered twenty-three thousand casualties.

When the war ended in 1865, Tennessee was in bad shape. Farms and railroads had been destroyed, and there was little money. People were exhausted from the war. However, Tennessee's people tackled

Bodies covered the ground and gunsmoke filled the air at the Battle of Shiloh. It was one of the bloodiest battles of the Civil War, killing twenty-three thousand men.

the job of healing their state. They rebuilt their railroads and got their farms working again. They brought in new industries and worked to improve education.

Into the Twentieth Century

The twentieth century brought new challenges. The country entered a depression in the 1930s. Money was tight everywhere and thousands of people were out of work. President Franklin Delano Roosevelt came up with a plan called the New Deal. He started large government programs that would create jobs. One agency that Roosevelt created was

Many famous country music stars have been proud to sing on the stage of the Grand Ole Opry House in Nashville. A weekly radio program, started in 1925, is broadcast from the theater.

the Tennessee Valley Authority. The TVA had the job of building dams along the Tennessee River to help control floods. Also, the power of the rushing river water could make electricity. The TVA brought electricity to thousands of people. For the first time, they could have electric lights, refrigerators, and washing machines.

Tennessee's citizens took pride in their state and their culture. They worked to make the Smoky Mountains a national park in 1934. Also, Tennesseans were busy making music. They played blues, country, gospel, bluegrass, and rock 'n' roll. This music had a huge influence on today's American music. Steadily, the people of Tennessee were creating a modern state.

Chapter 3

THE GOVERNMENT OF TENNESSEE

If there were no government, society would probably fall apart. The government makes laws so that people can live together. It also provides services such as public education and police protection.

Structure of Government

Tennessee's state government is similar to that of the national government. It has three branches. The legislative branch makes laws. The executive branch carries out the laws. The judicial branch makes sure people obey the laws. It also settles any disagreements.

The legislative branch of Tennessee has two parts. One is the Senate. The other is the House of Representatives. Together they are called the General Assembly. Voters in different districts elect people to the General Assembly. The House has ninety-nine representatives, and the Senate has thirty-three members.

To be a legislator (a senator or representative), a person must be a U.S. citizen. He or she must have lived in the state for at least three years and in the district for at least one year. Representatives must be at least twenty-one years old. Senators must be at least thirty. Representatives serve two years. Senators are elected for four-year terms.

A joint session of the state legislature—including both senators and representatives—was held in Nashville in 2009. Members gathered to listen to Governor Phil Bredesen.

To make a new law, Tennessee legislators first write a bill. This is like a first draft. Members of the General Assembly discuss the bill. They make changes if necessary. Then they vote. If a majority approves, the bill goes to the governor.

The governor is the head of the executive branch. When the governor gets a bill, he or she can sign it into law or veto it. The governor also oversees several departments. For example, there are departments for education, public health, agriculture, transportation, and tourism. To be governor, a person must be at least thirty years old. The governor must also be a U.S. citizen who has lived in Tennessee for seven years.

A system of courts makes up the judicial branch. People who are accused of crimes are tried in courts. A judge and jury listen to all of the facts. Then they decide who is right and wrong. They also decide what the punishment will be.

Local Governments

Everybody likes to do things differently. A law that works in one place might not make sense somewhere else. Local governments can make laws for the people in a smaller area.

A man takes a photo of the Washington County Courthouse in Jonesborough. Washington County was Tennessee's first county.

Besides the state government, Tennessee also has local governments for its cities and counties. The state has ninety-five counties. Each of them has a county commission. This is a group of people who work together to make the laws. County governments decide how county money will be spent. They also keep a lot of records. At the county courthouse, you can find out when people were born, when they got married, and whether they own any property.

Tennessee also has several city governments and metropolitan governments. These governments do things that are only needed in these areas. For example, they make rules about parking. They will decide where to build new stores or houses. Sometimes, a

The Tennessee Constitution

Past . . .

Government in Tennessee began when the first people crossed the Appalachian Mountains. These first settlers formed a community called Watauga.

They knew they needed a system to keep things running smoothly. In 1772, they formed the Watauga Association. Then they wrote the Articles of the Watauga Association. This is considered by some to be the first constitution written in the American colonies. It listed what people's rights were and what the rules of the society were. The settlers elected five people to run the government. There was also a clerk to keep records and a sheriff to maintain law and order.

Later, Tennessee became a state. Its citizens wrote a new constitution. Tennesseans believed that each person should have rights. The state's bill of rights is an important part of the constitution. The constitution also described how the government should be set up. Thomas Jefferson, who would later become president of the United States, was impressed with Tennessee's constitution. He said it was the most "republican" in the country. By this, he meant that it recognized the rights of its citizens.

Present . . .

Tennessee's constitution was amended in 1835 and again in 1870. Most of the 1870 version is still in use, but there are some changes. For example, in 1953, the constitution was amended to elect governors for four years. Before that, they had served for two years. Then in 1977, governors were allowed to serve two terms instead of one.

The constitution is not perfect. Some critics think it does not make public education important enough. It is not clear about how to collect taxes. However, the constitution is flexible. It has been through many changes.

metropolitan government is needed. A metropolitan government combines a city and county government. A county with a large city in it could have two different governments. They might both be doing the same thing, so by combining the two governments they are more efficient. In 1963, the government of Nashville combined with Davidson County. It was the first big city in the country to have a metropolitan government.

Government in Action

Throughout its history, Tennessee has had a big influence on national issues. In 1919, an amendment was proposed to the U.S. Constitution. It would give women the right to vote. Thirty-six states had to vote "yes" for it to pass. When the vote came to Tennessee, thirty-five states had passed the amendment. The vote in Tennessee was close: one lawmaker had been against the idea, but his mother encouraged him to support it. He voted yes. Tennessee was the deciding vote! Tennessee became the thirty-sixth state to pass the amendment, making it a national law.

Tennessee made headlines again in 1925. The state had passed a law that said schools could not teach the theory of evolution. In Dayton, Tennessee, science teacher John Scopes taught evolution anyway. He was arrested. In the trial, Scopes's lawyers challenged whether the law was constitutional. Scopes was found guilty. However, his conviction was set aside because the judge broke a rule regarding how Scopes should be sentenced. In the years to come, there were many disagreements about whether evolution should be taught in public schools. They are still going on today.

In 2000, the United States had a presidential election. Republican George W. Bush ran against Vice President Al Gore. Gore came from

Tennesseean Al Gore *(left)* served as vice president under President Bill Clinton in the 1990s. Gore ran for president in 2000, but he lost to George W. Bush *(right)* in a close race.

Tennessee. This race was perhaps the closest and most controversial in American history. Because of the way votes are counted, it is possible for a candidate to win the popular vote (the total number of votes) and still lose the election. This is exactly what happened to Gore. He won the popular vote by half a million votes, but he still lost the election. In an interesting twist, Gore did not win in his home state of Tennessee. If he had, he would have been president.

Chapter 4

THE ECONOMY OF TENNESSEE

No matter where you live, chances are good that some Tennessee product has touched your life. You might have clothes made from cotton that was grown in Tennessee. If you drink Coca-Cola, it might have come from a factory in Chattanooga. Your car may have been built in Tennessee, and the electricity that runs your lights may be produced there also.

Agriculture, Manufacturing, and Mining

Settlers who came to Tennessee saw that the land had many natural resources. There was good soil and a lot of wild game. During the Civil War, Tennessee was a national leader in growing food for hungry soldiers.

Tennessee does not have as much farmland as it used to. However, agriculture is still part of the state's economy. Some important crops are cotton, corn, soybeans, and tobacco. Cattle are another important part of the state's agricultural output.

Tennessee even has its own breed of horse. In the early 1800s, horsemen wanted an animal that could handle Tennessee's mountains. They bred the Tennessee walking horse. This horse is hardy,

Coal mining is vital to Tennessee's economy. It is also controversial, from environmental hazards to dangerous work conditions.

good-tempered, and has a smooth walk—perfect for the rough terrain.

Mining is another vital part of the state's economy. Coal comes out of East Tennessee. The state is the nation's second largest producer of zinc. Zinc is a metal used to cover and protect other metals. It is also found in vitamins.

Limestone, sandstone, and marble are also found in Tennessee. These are used in houses and buildings. Ball clay, abundant in northwest Tennessee, is a type of clay used to make dishes and tiles.

Manufacturing contributes a lot to Tennessee's economy. Throughout the state, factories turn out automobiles, chemicals, and metal products. Processed foods and drinks are also made here.

Service Industries

Service industries make up most of Tennessee's economy. These industries do not make actual things—like cars or cotton. Instead, they provide services. Education, health care, insurance, and

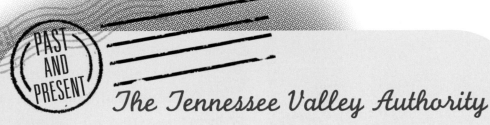

The Tennessee Valley Authority

Past . . .

President Franklin D. Roosevelt created the Tennessee Valley Authority in 1933. The TVA was part of the "New Deal." The New Deal was Roosevelt's plan to jump-start the nation's economy during the Great Depression. The TVA would create jobs for people who badly needed them. The "authority" of the TVA was not just in Tennessee. It also covered parts of Alabama, Mississippi, Kentucky, Virginia, Georgia, and North Carolina.

The TVA's job was to manage Tennessee's rivers. Engineers would build dams to create lakes and reservoirs. These would help control flooding. These lakes would also provide a place for people to go swimming, fishing, and boating. The dams had another important use. Rushing water is a very powerful force. By harnessing its power, the TVA was able to create electricity. This electricity brought power to thousands of homes in Tennessee and other states.

Present . . .

Many people still get electricity from the TVA. It is one of the largest producers of electrical power in the nation.

The TVA has always been controversial. Although it created jobs, the TVA projects cut through the heart of Tennessee. Some farmers lost their land because the TVA needed it. Some people said a government agency should not make power. They thought that job should go to private companies. Even today, some people criticize the agency for being too big and powerful.

The TVA came under fire in December 2008. The agency had a pond that held wet coal ash. The ash is a waste product from coal mining. A wall of the pond broke, and tons of coal ash spread over hundreds of acres. People were worried about the pollution to the land and water. The TVA began a huge cleanup, but environmental groups threatened to sue the agency.

A turnstile and the word "Entrance" greet customers ready to shop the well-stocked shelves of a Piggly Wiggly in Memphis in 1917.

government services fall into this category. Teachers, doctors, police officers, and store clerks are all service workers.

The city of Memphis is home to two well-known service businesses. In 1916, a man named Clarence Saunders opened a grocery store. He called it Piggly Wiggly. Before the arrival of Piggly Wiggly, shoppers told the clerk what they wanted and then waited while the clerk gathered up their items. Piggly Wiggly was different. There, customers found their own groceries. This self-service idea was radically different.

In 1971, another kind of service business started in Memphis. Frederick W. Smith wanted to find a faster way to deliver packages. He formed a company in order to accomplish this task. On one night in 1973, it delivered 186 packages overnight. Today, Smith's company—FedEx—delivers more than seven million pieces of mail each and every day.

Country music singer Dolly Parton waves to fans as she rides in an antique car during an appearance at Dollywood. Parton owns the popular East Tennessee theme park.

Another important service industry is tourism. Many visitors to Tennessee want to take advantage of its natural assets. The Smoky Mountains became a national park in 1934. With almost ten million visitors per year, it is now the most popular in the national park system.

One quirky attraction is at the Peabody Hotel in Memphis. In 1933, two men put some ducks in the hotel's fountain. It was just a joke, but people loved the ducks. Soon there were ducks living there all the time. Now, each day the ducks march through the hotel lobby to the fountain at 11 AM. They leave at 5 PM. A special "duckmaster" teaches the ducks how to march and takes them to and from their home on the roof in a special elevator.

If there is one thing Tennessee is known for, it's music. Thousands of tourists who visit Tennessee come because they are interested in music. From East Tennessee came gospel and bluegrass. From Middle Tennessee came country music. From Memphis came the blues and rock'n'roll.

Nashville is known as the country music capital of the United States. The city's music industry is worth about $6 billion. Tourists in Nashville might stroll down Music Row, where there are many businesses that serve the music industry. They can also visit the Country Music Hall of Fame.

Music fans in East Tennessee can go to Dollywood. This is a theme park started by country music star Dolly Parton. It is near Pigeon Forge, Tennessee.

Tourists can continue the journey in Memphis. On Beale Street, they can see the nightclubs where famous blues musicians played. Sun Records is also located in Memphis. Legends like Elvis Presley, Johnny Cash, Carl Perkins, and Jerry Lee Lewis recorded their classics at the Sun studios.

Presley's former home is also in Memphis. Graceland is a large, ostentatious mansion where tourists can get a glimpse of Presley's life.

Chapter 5

PEOPLE FROM TENNESSEE: PAST AND PRESENT

More than six million people live in Tennessee. About 80 percent of them are white. Another 17 percent are black. The rest are American Indians, Asians, and members of other ethnic groups. About two-thirds of Tennessee's residents live in cities or towns. The rest live in rural areas.

No matter what they look like or where they live, the people of Tennessee are proud of their state and its heritage.

Heroes of All Kinds

The Tennessee mountains were home to rugged mountain men. David Crockett was one of the most famous of these men. A popular folk song says he was born on a mountaintop. However, he was probably born in a cabin in Eastern Tennessee. Crockett wasn't good in school, but he learned how to live off the land. He fought with Andrew Jackson in the War of 1812. He also represented Tennessee in the U.S. House of Representatives. Crockett later moved to Texas. There, he fought in the Mexican-American War and died a hero in 1836 at the famous Battle of the Alamo.

Years later, Tennessee produced another war hero. Alvin York, from Pall Mall, Tennessee, fought in World War I. He was one of nine

Americans who captured 132 enemy soldiers. York was called the greatest American hero of the war.

Casey Jones, born in Jackson, Tennessee, was a railroad engineer. In 1900, he was driving a passenger train south from Memphis. On the tracks ahead, a freight train blocked his way. It was too late to stop. However, Jones braked hard and slowed down to about 35 miles (56 km) per hour by the time the two trains crashed. Jones died instantly—and became a hero. By slowing the train down, he saved the lives of all his passengers.

Wilma Rudolph was a different kind of hero. She proved that people could achieve their

With his coonskin cap, rifle, and dogs, David Crockett was ready to live off the land in the late 1700s and early 1800s.

dreams. Rudolph was an African American woman born in 1940. As a child, Rudolph had polio. This disease makes it hard to walk. Rudolph got better and became a track-and-field star in high school and college. She went on to the Olympics, where she won three gold medals in 1960. She had a homecoming parade in her hometown of Clarksville, Tennessee. Rudolph insisted that both whites and blacks be allowed to attend. It was the town's first integrated event.

Tina Turner sings onstage in the early 1970s. Combining rock, soul, and rhythm and blues, Turner gave powerful and energetic performances that earned her millions of fans.

Musicians

Tennessee is the home of country music and the birthplace of the blues. It's no wonder that a lot of musicians have lived here.

Elvis Presley, called the King of Rock 'n' Roll, moved to Tennessee when he was thirteen. His music mixed gospel and blues with a harder beat. Young Americans in the 1950s loved it. Presley built his famous home, Graceland, in Memphis. He lived there until he died in 1977.

Tina Turner is sometimes called the Queen of Rock 'n' Roll. She was born in Nutbush, Tennessee. Turner's music is a combination of rock and soul. She has won numerous major awards.

The Melungeons: People of a Mysterious Past

Past....

Who were the Melungeons? Were they black? White? Indian? Something else? Nobody seems to know. This group of people did not seem to fit into any specific racial category. There were theories that they might be Portuguese or Spanish. Perhaps they were from the Mediterranean or the Middle East. Anthropologists in the first half of the twentieth century studied the Melungeons, but could not figure out where they came from. Wherever they came from, the Melungeons kept to themselves in the mountains of East Tennessee.

It is not even certain where the term "Melungeon" is from. One theory is that it comes from a French word—*mélange*—meaning "mixture."

Other people tended to shun the Melungeons. It used to be that only white Tennesseans could vote. This left out the Melungeons. When children misbehaved, their parents might tell them that the Melungeons would "get them." The term was used as a racial insult, as well as a political one.

By the 1960s, it seemed that the Melungeon population was shrinking. However, the Melungeons started to show pride in their heritage. A drama group put on a successful play about the Melungeons called *Walk Toward the Sunset*.

Present....

Anthropologists continued to research the Melungeons throughout the 1980s and 1990s. Recent DNA testing has revealed that the Melungeons were mostly white. They had elements of Native American and African American blood. They were descended from parts of Europe, as well as the Mediterranean, Turkey, and India.

In 1997, a group of Melungeons organized a meeting. Because it was the first modern gathering of Melungeon people, they called it the First Union. They expected about fifty people to come. Instead, about six hundred people showed up! In 1998, the Melungeon Heritage Association was born.

Carl Perkins, from Tiptonville, Tennessee, was known as the King of Rockabilly. He listened to the early stars of Nashville on the radio. He made a homemade guitar and learned to play. Soon, he was writing songs. Perkins went to Memphis to start a career in music. His song "Blue Suede Shoes" became a huge hit.

From the eastern part of the state came Dolly Parton, one of the greatest country singers of all time. Parton was one of twelve children born into a poor family in Sevierville, Tennessee. She started performing as a child. She went on to write and record dozens of popular songs and has even had roles in movies.

Carl Perkins was a talented singer and songwriter who worked with people like Elvis Presley, Johnny Cash, and Jerry Lee Lewis.

Other Tennessee musicians were blues singers W. C. Handy and Bessie Smith. Country music legends Roy Acuff and Kitty Wells also came from Tennessee.

Writers and Actors

Several writers come from Tennessee. Cormac McCarthy and James Agee both won the Pulitzer Prize for literature. Another author, Alex

In this portrait, Cherokee Indian Sequoyah points to the alphabet he invented so that the Cherokee people would have a form of written communication.

Haley, won a special Pulitzer for his book *Roots*, which tells the story of an African American family. It was loosely based on Haley's own family history and was published in thirty-seven languages and made into a TV movie.

One of Tennessee's most important writers never actually published a book. Sequoyah was a Cherokee Indian born in the mid-1700s. At the time, the Cherokee had no written language. Sequoyah was interested in how white men communicated using marks on paper. He thought these "talking leaves" were a good idea! Sequoyah worked for twelve years to develop a Cherokee alphabet. As a result, thousands of Cherokee learned to read and write.

Actors Samuel L. Jackson and Morgan Freeman are also from Tennessee. Oprah Winfrey moved there when she was fourteen. It's where she got her start at local radio and TV stations. Later, she got her own show—and became the richest woman in America.

Many famous people have left their mark on Tennessee. However, the state's character does not come from just a handful of people. It comes from the people who had the courage and stamina to settle the land. It comes from the people who put their ideas and talents to work. And it comes from the people who live there now, working to build its future.

1540	Spanish explorer Hernando de Soto reaches Tennessee.
1772	The Watauga Association writes its own constitution.
1775–1783	The American Revolution is fought.
1784	The state of Franklin is formed.
1796	Tennessee becomes a state.
1811	The New Madrid Earthquake forms Reelfoot Lake.
1812	Tennessee earns the nickname the Volunteer State.
1829	Andrew Jackson becomes president of the United States.
1838	Thousands of Cherokee are forced to leave Tennessee and go to Oklahoma on the Trail of Tears.
1861	Tennessee is the last state to secede from the Union before the Civil War.
1865	The Civil War ends; the Ku Klux Klan is formed in Pulaski, Tennessee.
1866	Tennessee becomes the first state to reenter the Union.
1870	Tennessee's constitution is revised.
1920	Tennessee becomes the thirty-sixth state to pass a constitutional amendment giving women the right to vote.
1925	Dayton, Tennessee, is the site of the famous Scopes "monkey trial."
1933	President Franklin D. Roosevelt establishes the Tennessee Valley Authority.
1968	Martin Luther King Jr. is assassinated in Memphis.
1982	The World's Fair is held in Knoxville.
1996	Tennessee becomes the first state to have all of its public schools connected to the Internet.
2000	Tennessean Al Gore runs for president of the United States.
2008	The state teams up with automobile maker Nissan to study how to introduce transportation systems that will handle electric cars.

Tennessee at a Glance

State motto	"Agriculture and commerce"
State capital	Nashville
State flower	Iris (state wildflower is the passionflower)
State bird	Mockingbird
State tree	Tulip poplar
State fruit	Tomato
Statehood date and number	June 1, 1796; sixteenth state
State nickname	Volunteer State
Total area and U.S. rank	42,146 square miles (109,157 sq km); thirty-sixth largest state
Population	6,156,000
Highest elevation	Clingman's Dome, 6,643 feet (2,024 m)
Lowest elevation	A spot in Shelby County, 182 feet (55 m)

State Flag

State Seal

Major rivers	Tennessee River, Mississippi River, Cumberland River
Major lake	Reelfoot Lake
Hottest temperature recorded	113 degrees Fahrenheit (45 degrees Celsius) at Perryville on July 29, 1930 and August 9, 1930
Coldest temperature recorded	-32°F (-35°C) at Mountain View on December 30, 1917
Origin of state name	Named after the Cherokee village of Tanasi, located on the Tennessee River; means "bend in the river"
Chief agricultural products	Cotton, corn, tobacco, soybeans
Major industries	Chemicals, automobiles, food products, services

Mockingbird

Iris

GLOSSARY

amendment A change.

bill A proposal for a new law.

biodiverse Having a variety of plants and animals.

casualty A death or injury resulting from a battle.

colony A territory governed by another country; often not physically connected.

dam A wall built to hold back water.

depression When the economy is extremely slow, characterized by high unemployment and not enough money.

evolution A scientific theory that says the human species developed directly from earlier primates (apes).

fertile Able to sustain much growth.

integrated Including people of all races.

ostentatious Extremely fancy or gaudy.

plantation A large farm requiring many workers, usually in the South.

plateau A hill or mountain with a flat top, like a table.

rockabilly A mix of rock 'n' roll and hillbilly (early country) music.

rugged Extremely tough or sturdy.

secede To break away.

shroud To cover or hide.

shun To refuse to associate with.

spelunker A person who explores caves.

stamina The ability to keep going.

term The period of time that an elected official serves in office.

Country Music Hall of Fame and Museum

222 Fifth Avenue South

Nashville, TN 37203

(615) 416-2001

E-mail: info@countrymusichalloffame.com

Web site: www.countrymusichalloffame.com

The Country Music Hall of Fame exists to preserve the history of country music and educate people about its influence.

Department of Economic and Community Development

312 Rosa L. Parks Avenue, 11th Floor

Nashville, TN 37243

(615) 741-1888

E-mail: ECD.communications.office@state.tn.us

Web site: http://www.state.tn.us/ecd

The department works to attract business and industry to Tennessee.

Department of Environment and Conservation

L&C Annex, 1st Floor

401 Church Street

Nashville, TN 37243

(615) 532-0109 or (888) 891-8332

E-mail: ask.tdec@state.tn.us

Web site: http://www.tdec.net

The department works to protect people from environmental dangers and to improve the quality of Tennessee's land and water. It also manages Tennessee's state parks.

Department of Tourist Development

312 Rosa L. Parks Avenue, 25th Floor

Nashville, TN 37243

(615) 741-2159

E-mail: tourdev@tn.gov

Web site: http://www.state.tn.us/tourdev

With a goal of promoting travel within the state, this department has information about natural, historical, and cultural tourist attractions.

Governor's Office

Tennessee State Capitol

600 Charlotte

Nashville, TN 37219

(615) 741-2001

E-mail: phil.bredsen@state.tn.us

Web site: http://www.tennesseeanytime.org/governor

This office provides information about the government of Tennessee.

Great Smoky Mountains National Park

107 Park Headquarters Road

Gatlinburg, TN 37738

(865) 436-1200

Web site: http://www.nps.gov/grsm/index.htm

This national park's headquarters offers information on the natural history and resources of the Smoky Mountains.

Tennessee Historical Commission

2941 Lebanon Road

Nashville, TN 37243

(615) 532-1550

Web site: http://www.tennessee.gov/environment/hist

The Tennessee Historical Commission encourages the study of the state's history and preserves historical sites.

Tennessee State Museum

505 Deaderick Street

Nashville, TN 37243

(615) 741-2692 or (800) 407-4324

E-mail: museuminfo@tnmuseum.org

Web site: www.tnmuseum.org

Through exhibits and education, the Tennessee State Museum preserves and promotes Tennessee history.

University of Tennessee

Knoxville, TN 37996

(865) 974-1000

E-mail: utnews@utk.edu

Web site: http://www.tennessee.edu

Departments at the university provide information and resources about many different aspects of Tennessee, such as history, geography, geology, and business.

Web Sites

Due to the changing nature of Internet links, Rosen Publishing has developed an online list of Web sites related to the subject of this book. This site is updated regularly. Please use this link to access the list:

http://www.rosenlinks.com/uspp/tnpp

FOR FURTHER READING

Barrett, Tracy. *Tennessee*. Tarrytown, NY: Benchmark, 2006.

Brands, H.W. *Andrew Jackson: His Life and Times*. New York, NY: Anchor, 2006.

Ernst, Kathleen. *Hearts of Stone*. New York, NY: Dutton Juvenile, 2006.

Graves, Renee. *The Scopes Trial*. New York, NY: Children's Press, 2007.

Guy, Joe. *The Hidden History of East Tennessee*. Charleston, SC: History Press, 2008.

Hama, Larry. *Surprise Attack!: Battle of Shiloh*. New York, NY: Osprey Publishing, 2006.

Ivey, Jennie, Calvin Dickinson, and Lisa Rand. *Tennessee Tales the Textbooks Don't Tell*. Johnson City, TN: Overmountain Press, 2002.

Lovett, Bobby L. *The Civil Rights Movement in Tennessee: A Narrative History*. Knoxville, TN: University of Tennessee Press, 2005.

Marrin, Albert. *Old Hickory: Andrew Jackson and the American People*. New York, NY: Dutton Juvenile, 2004.

Meacham, Jon. *American Lion: Andrew Jackson in the White House*. New York, NY: Random House, 2009.

Moonshower, Candie. *The Legend of Zoey*. New York, NY: Delacorte Books for Young Readers, 2006.

Oermann, Robert K. *Behind the Grand Ole Opry Curtain: Tales of Romance and Tragedy*. New York, NY: Center Street, 2008.

Olwell, Russell B. *At Work in the Atomic City: A Labor and Social History of Oak Ridge*. Knoxville, TN: University of Tennessee Press, 2009.

Parks, Aileen Wells. *Davy Crockett: Young Rifleman*. New York, NY: Aladdin, 2009.

Parton, Dolly. *Dolly: My Life and Other Unfinished Business*. New York, NY: HarperCollins, 1995.

Petreycik, Rick. *It's My State: Tennessee*. Tarrytown, NY: Marshall Cavendish, 2006.

Rumford, James. *Sequoyah: The Cherokee Man Who Gave His People Writing*. Boston, MA: Houghton Mifflin, 2004.

Victor, Adam. *The Elvis Encyclopedia*. New York, NY: Overlook Press, 2008.

Winkler, Wayne. *Walking Toward the Sunset: The Melungeons of Appalachia*. Macon, GA: Mercer University Press, 2005.

Wisler, G. Clifton. *Thunder on the Tennessee*. New York, NY: Puffin, 1995.

BIBLIOGRAPHY

Chapman, Jefferson. "Prehistoric American Indians in Tennessee." McClungmuseum.utk. edu. Research Notes 27 (2009). Retrieved February 27, 2009 (http://mcclungmuseum. utk.edu/research/renotes/rn-27txt.htm).

Crawford, Charles W. *Dynamic Tennessee: Land, History, and Government*. Austin, TX: Steck-Vaughn Company, 1990.

Faulkner, Charles H. "Four Thousand Years of Native American Cave Art in the Southern Appalachians." *Journal of Cave and Karst Studies*, December (1997): 148–153.

Lacey, T. Jensen. *Amazing Tennessee*. Nashville, TN: Rutledge Hill Press, 2000.

Lyons, William. *Government and Politics in Tennessee*. Knoxville, TN: The University of Tennessee Press, 2001.

Speer, Ed. *The Tennessee Handbook*. Jefferson, NC: McFarland and Company, Inc., 2002.

Tennessee Department of Environment and Conservation. "Tennessee's Mineral Industry." Retrieved February 11, 2009 (http://www.state.tn.us/environment/tdg/ mineralind.shtml).

Travel and History. "Tennessee Valley Authority." Retrieved February 24, 2009 (http:// www.u-s-history.com/pages/h1653.html).

TVA.gov. "From the New Deal to a New Century." Retrieved February 12, 2009 (http:// www.tva.gov/abouttva/history.htm).

University of Virginia Miller Center of Public Affairs. "Andrew Jackson: A Life in Brief." Retrieved February 10, 2009 (http://millercenter.org/academic/americanpresident/ jackson/essays/biography/1).

Van West, Carroll, ed. *The Tennessee Encyclopedia of History and Culture*. Nashville, TN: Rutledge Hill Press, 1998.

Weeks, Terry, and Bob Womack. *Tennessee: The History of an American State*. Montgomery, AL: Clairmont Press, 1996.

Winkler, Wayne. "A Brief Overview of the Melungeons." Melungeons.com. Retrieved February 11, 2009 (http://www.melungeons.com/articles/jan2003.htm).

Zimmerman, Peter Coats. *Tennessee Music: Its People and Places*. San Francisco, CA: Miller Freeman Books, 1998.

INDEX

A

Acuff, Roy, 35
African Americans, rights for, 5, 14
Agee, James, 35
Appalachian Mountains, 5–7, 12, 22

C

caves, 22
Civil War, 5, 16–17, 25
constitution, of Tennessee, 22
Country Music Hall of Fame, 30
Crockett, David, 31

E

evolution, controversy on teaching
    theory of, 23

F

Freeman, Morgan, 37

G

Gore, Al, 23–24

H

Haley, Alex, 35–36
Handy, W. C., 35

J

Jackson, Andrew, 15–16, 31
Jackson, Samuel L., 37
Jones, Casey, 32

M

McCarthy, Cormac, 35
Melungeons, 34

P

Parton, Dolly, 30, 35
Perkins, Carl, 30, 35
Presley, Elvis, 30, 33

R

Reelfoot Lake, 8–9
Rudolph, Wilma, 32

S

Sequoyah, 36–37
Smith, Bessie, 35
Smoky Mountains, 7, 11, 18
Sun Records, 30

T

Tennessee
    economy of, 5, 25–30
    geography of, 6–11
    government of, 19–24
    history of, 5, 7, 12–18
    people from, 31–37
Tennessee Valley Authority, 18, 27
Turner, Tina, 33

W

Wells, Kitty, 35
Winfrey, Oprah, 37

Y

York, Alvin, 31–32

About the Author

Diane Bailey is an Oklahoma native who has visited Tennessee several times. She is a fan of the traditional American music that got its start in Tennessee, and she enjoys learning how history and culture have shaped our country today. Now, she lives in Kansas and writes on a variety of nonfiction topics.

Photo Credits

Designer: Les Kanturek; Editor: Bethany Bryan
Photo Researcher: Amy Feinberg